COLOURFUL TRAVELS

Sights of CANADA

ALBERTA

BARBARA JANMAN

Enjoy Your Travels

Barb Janman 2017

FriesenPress

Suite 300 - 990 Fort St
Victoria, BC, V8V 3K2
Canada

www.friesenpress.com

ISBN
978-1-4602-9017-0 (Paperback)

1. TRAVEL, CANADA, WESTERN PROVINCES (AB, BC)

Distributed to the trade by The Ingram Book Company

INTRODUCTION

TRAVEL ADDS THE FOURTH DIMENSION TO MY LIFE

I grew up in a variety of places in western Canada, from the foothills to the prairie wheat fields. My nomadic and very interesting life provided exposure to many different cultures and experiences which formed my wanderlust for travel and my desire to share these experiences with you.

I love the excitement of seeing new dimensions and being able to use my imagination to create the spaces.

THIS BOOK IS ABOUT HAVING FUN WHILE YOU TRAVEL !!

This is the third in my series of colouring books, scrapbooks and journaling books combined, they all tell a story about the sights and travel in CANADA.

I have captured only a small number of interesting places there are to see in these areas of our Country. Again, I urge you to enjoy as many places and events as possible on your journey. Some short stories or comments of who, what, where, when and/or why are written opposite the drawings, this will introduce you to the scene. The blank spaces are meant for you to add your own photographs and to write your story of fun.

This book may, at your discretion, become a scrap book for your trip, record the 5 w's and include your thoughts about what you see and do. All drawings are awaiting your embellishments, add to the drawings, make them your own. Using pencils will allow you to add dimension, shading, blending and create more patterns of your choosing.

THE RICHNESS OF TRAVEL IS IN THE FRIENDS YOU MEET

This book is dedicated to my family, especially my husband, Bill, and my friends, without their support this project would not have been possible. I am so very grateful for their contributions of picture suggestions, their assistance in reading the text, and co-ordination of activities and their encouragement.

Thank you all, I love you........ Barbara Janman

Please enjoy your *"Colourful Travels"* through the pages

WEBSITE: Colourfultravels.com
EMAIL: Info@colourfultravels.com
Produced and printed in Canada

THIS BOOK BELONGS TO

_____

DATE _____

ALBERTA is a western province of Canada with an approximate population of 4,200,000 as of 2016. Our land-locked province was established in September 1905.

Edmonton is the capital city of Alberta and is located near the geographical centre of the province. It has been known as the oil capital and is the primary supply depot for the northern resource industries such as oil extraction, mining, forestry, and general construction.

Calgary, in the southern part of the province, is the largest city in area as well as population.

Alberta enjoys many days of sunshine annually, upward of 2,500 hours/year in the Medicine Hat area and Jasper has just short of 2,000 hours of sunshine per year. It has been my experience that the climate is somewhat arid, with moderate winter weather. The warm Chinook winds provide a pleasurable break in the cold of winter in the southern part of the province. You will often hear Albertans say, "Gee, its cold today." "Yes, but it's a dry cold," or "wait twenty minutes and the weather will change." One thing is for sure, if you are going out for the day, take a jacket.

There are many interesting places to see and events to attend while visiting Alberta. Tourist destinations include Banff, Canmore, Lake Louise, Jasper, Waterton Lakes, Lethbridge, Crowsnest Pass, Medicine Hat, Brooks, Drumheller, Red Deer, Sylvan Lake, there are really far too many to list here.[1]

My story

_____

_____

_____

_____

_____

_____

_____

My photos / doodles / sketches

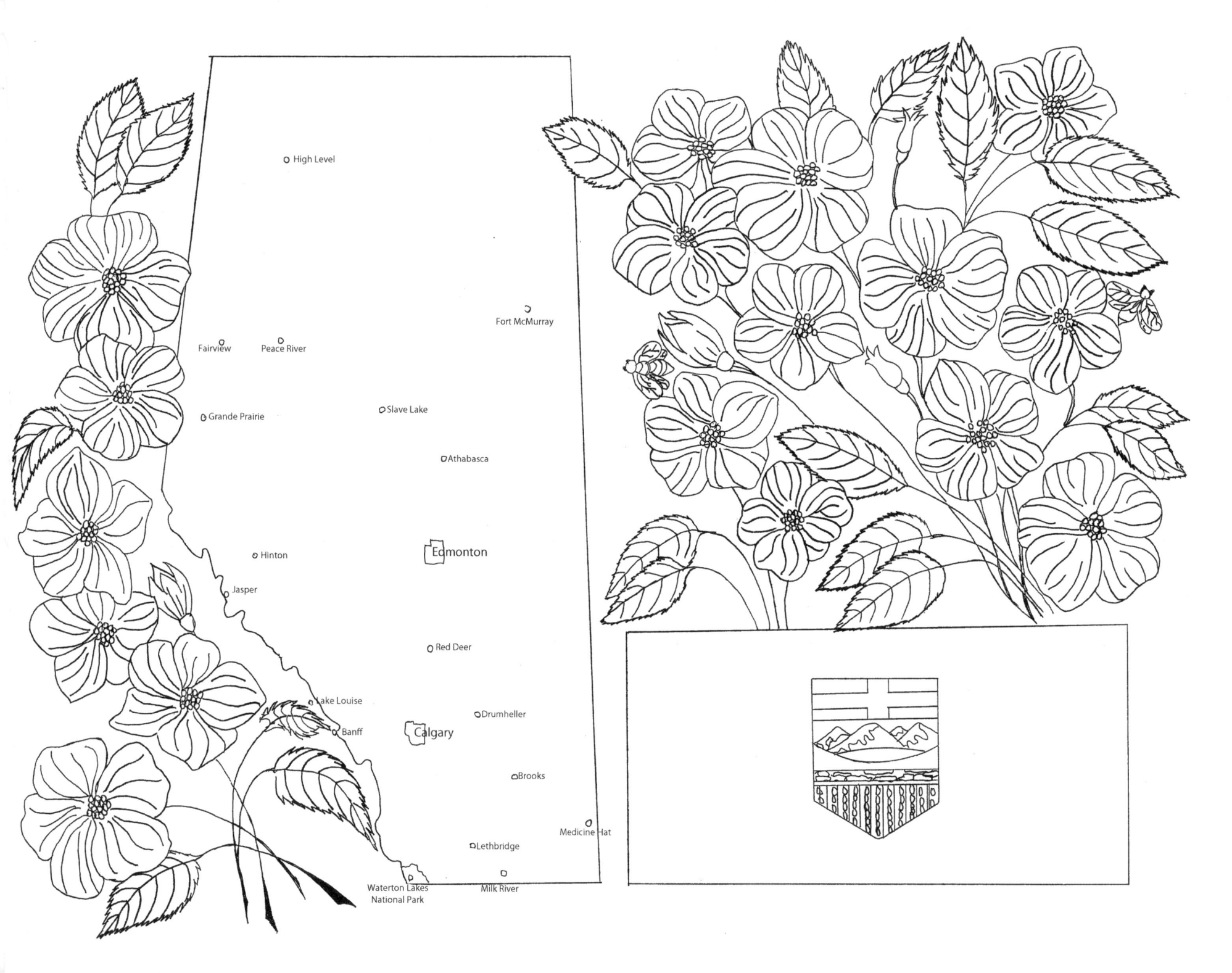

High Level

Fort McMurray

Fairview Peace River

Grande Prairie Slave Lake

Athabasca

Hinton Edmonton

Jasper

Red Deer

Lake Louise

Drumheller

Banff Calgary

Brooks

Medicine Hat

Lethbridge

Waterton Lakes Milk River
National Park

Scenery of Alberta

The Three Sisters

The Three Sisters are a trio of peaks in the Rocky Mountain range near Canmore, Alberta, Canada. They are known individually as Big Sister (Faith), Middle Sister (Charity), and Little Sister (Hope).

It was Albert Rogers, a nephew of Major Rogers, the discoverer of Rogers Pass in the Selkirk Mountains, who named the three peaks in 1883. He recalled, "There had been quite a heavy snowstorm in the night, and when we got up in the morning and looked out of the tent I noticed each of the three peaks had a heavy veil of snow on the north side and I said to the boys, 'Look at the Three Nuns.' They were called the Three Nuns for quite a while but later were called the 'Three Sisters,' more Protestant like I suppose." The name Three Sisters first appeared on Dr. George Dawson's map of 1886 and it is quite likely he who thought that the name Three Sisters would be more appropriate.

In the traditional language of the Îyârhe Nakoda (Stoney), the peaks are also referred to as the three sisters. However, the name refers to a story of Î-ktomnî, the old man, or trickster, who would promise three sisters in marriage whenever he was in trouble.

If you are staying in the area, there are many excellent hiking trails for you to explore.[2]

My story

_____

_____

_____

_____

_____

_____

_____

My photos / doodles / sketches

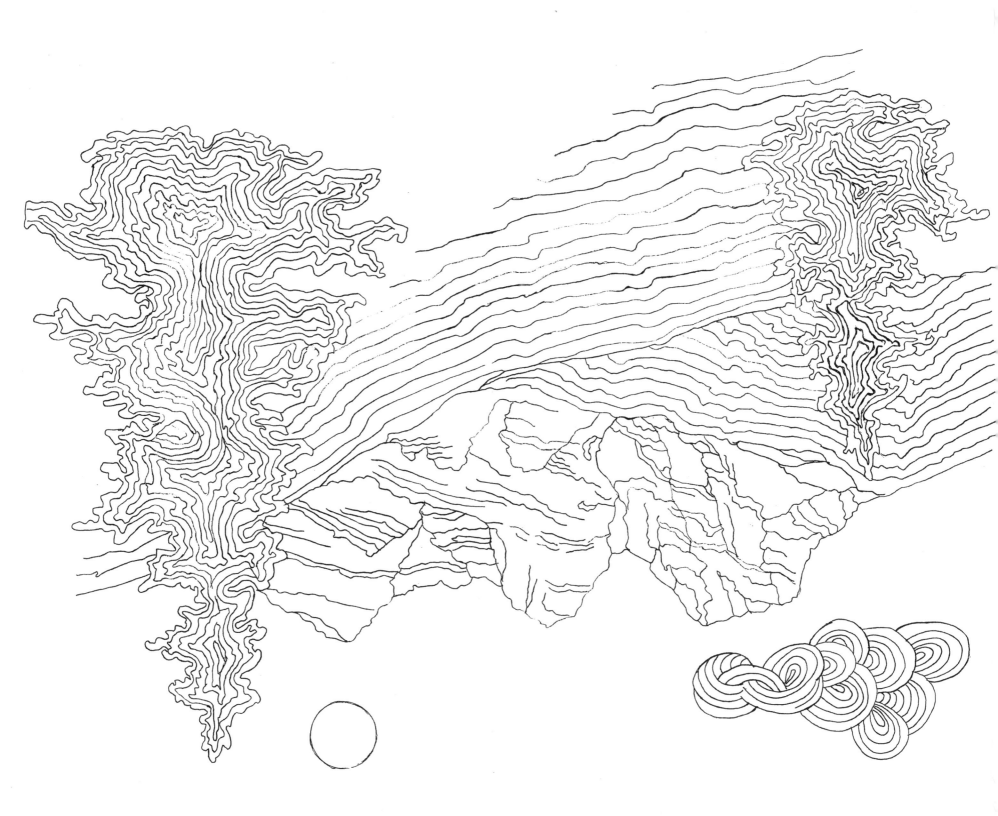

Lake Louise

The hamlet is named for the nearby Lake Louise, which in turn was named after Princess Louise Caroline Alberta (1848-1939), the fourth daughter of Queen Victoria and the wife of John Campbell, the 9th Duke of Argyll, who was the Governor General of Canada from 1878 to 1883. The hamlet was originally called Laggan and was a station along the Canadian Pacific Railway route built in 1890. The railway station building was preserved and moved into Heritage Park in Calgary.

The village is mainly made up of a small shopping centre, which includes a deli, bakery, grill, and other boutique shops. The Chateau Lake Louise is perched just back from the shore of Lake Louise. The beautiful green colour of the lake comes from glacial run off, it's an emerald in the Rockies.

The lake is surrounded by mountainous peaks; Mount Temple, Mount Whyte, and Mount Niblock are all above 2,975 meters (approximately 9,760 feet).

Icelandic poppies are beautiful and abundant through spring and early summer.

While visiting Lake Louise you have many activities to enjoy including hiking and canoeing and in the winter you can ski or enjoy the ice sculptures and always enjoy a cup of hot chocolate in the lodge.[3]

My story

_____

_____

_____

_____

_____

_____

_____

My photos / doodles / sketches

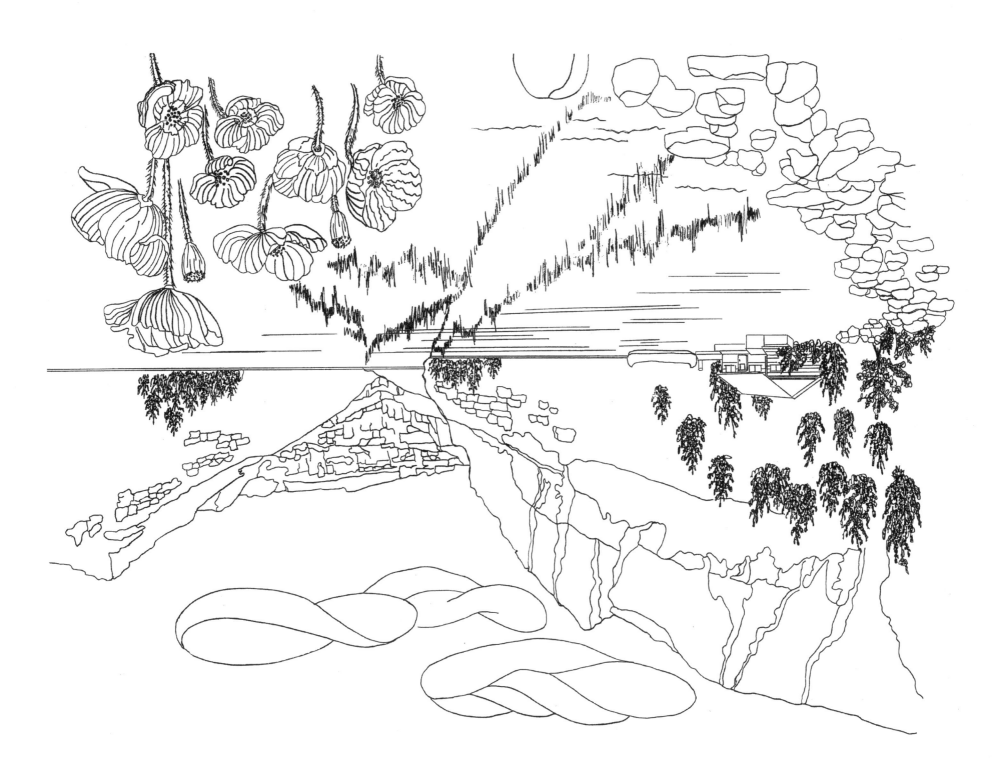

Prairie Fields and Agriculture

Alberta has built an international reputation as a reliable source of agricultural technology, expertise, and food. With 50 million acres used for crop and livestock production, Alberta produces an abundant supply of agricultural commodities available for export and as input for Alberta's processed food products. Along with almost 40 per cent of Canada's beef cattle, Alberta produces plentiful supplies of grain, dairy products, pork, poultry, vegetables, sugar, cooking oils, and honey.

Barley, wheat, legumes, alfalfa, mixed grains, canola, fruits, and berries are all grown in Alberta.

Most farming takes place in eastern and north-central Alberta.

My story

_____

_____

_____

_____

_____

_____

_____

My photos / doodles / sketches

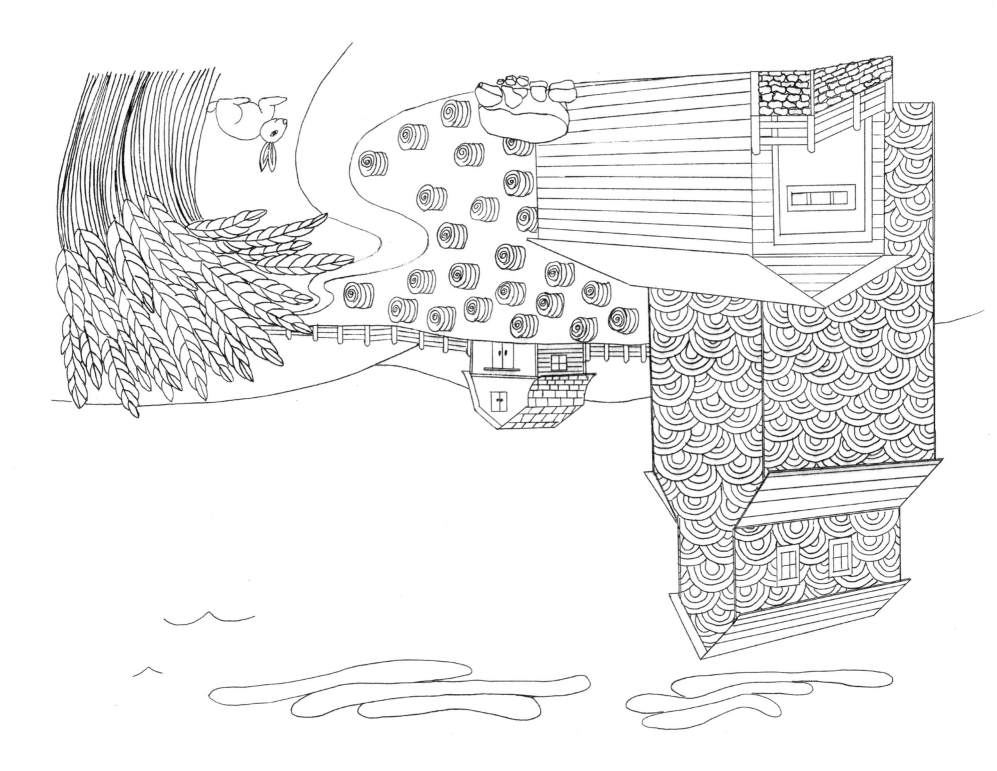

Drumheller Area

Drumheller is a town (formerly a city) within the Red Deer River valley in the badlands of east-central Alberta. It is located 110 kilometres (68 miles) northeast of Calgary. The Drumheller portion of the Red Deer River valley, often referred to as Dinosaur Valley, has an approximate width of 2 kilometres (1.2 miles) and an approximate length of 28 kilometres (17 miles).

Drumheller has been the filming location for more than 50 commercials, television, and cinematic productions including Running Brave, MythQuest, Unforgiven, ABC's miniseries Dreamkeeper, and TNT's miniseries Into the West.

The attraction to Drumheller for me is the total fantasy of prehistoric creatures roaming "our" local landscape. Open your mind, survey the terrain, close your eyes, and imagine the dinosaurs grazing and hunting through the valley. Amazing

The Royal Tyrell Museum of Paleontology has Canada's largest display of dinosaur fossils. Follow the road signs, you can't miss it.

Go find the bones, the hipbone is connected to the leg bone...♪♪♪

My story

_____

_____

_____

_____

_____

_____

_____

My photos / doodles / sketches

Around Drumheller

Not far from Drumheller is a small town named Rosebud, known for fine professional live theatre productions.

North of Drumheller is **Rowley,** an authentic ghost town.

North and west of Rowley is Red Deer, where the Alberta Sports Hall of Fame and the Kerry Wood Nature Centre reside.

Points of interest west of Red Deer:

The Beaver Boardwalk in Hinton

William A Switzer Provincial Park

The Icefields Parkway highway tour

Nordegg's Heritage Museum Centre and Brazeau Collieries Mine Site

My story

_____

_____

_____

_____

_____

_____

_____

_____

My photos / doodles / sketches

Southern Alberta

Worth a visit:

Dinosaur Provincial Park, Drive Cowboy Trail (Hwy 22) through high ranch country. In the summer, stay on a guest ranch and herd real cattle with real cowboys. Go horseback riding and whitewater rafting in the mountains, hike, paddle, or ride just about anywhere in the Crowsnest Pass.

Writing on Stone Provincial Park about 100 kms southeast of Lethbridge; known for a large number of aboriginal rock carvings and paintings.

Explore the shady past and funky arts scene of Lethbridge. Discover the massive 1907 coal mining operation of the Leitch Collieries and witness the devastation caused by the 1903 Frank Slide.

Visit Vulcan to celebrate its Trekcetera Museum.
Nanton is the home of the Bomber Command Museum.
Lethbridge offers Escape from LA, Henderson Lake, Nikka Yuko Japanese Gardens, and the Galt Museum.
Waterton Lakes National Park is located 90 minutes southwest of Lethbridge.
Cypress Hills Interprovincial Park is situated 32 km (20 miles) southeast of Medicine Hat.
Head-Smashed-In Buffalo Jump is an hour west of Lethbridge.
Bar U Ranch is 90 minutes southwest of Calgary.
Coal Mining History, Atlas Coal Mine National Historic Site, is 15 minutes southeast of Drumheller.

Also visit Elkwater to enjoy coal mining history at its best. In Milk River paddle or float along while admiring the canyons, cliffs, and gullies of the Badlands. Take a picture of Alberta's very last row of wooden grain elevators in nearby Warner, 45 minutes southeast of Lethbridge.[4]

My story

_____

_____

_____

_____

_____

_____

My photos / doodles / sketches

More of Southern Alberta

The Old Man Dam was built in 1992 to alleviate the drought situation for the agricultural industry in southern Alberta.

In addition to the new agricultural industry provided by the building of the dam, southern Alberta now has exceptional recreational facilities for camping, fishing, power boating, water skiing, wind surfing, canoeing, kayaking, sailing, wildlife viewing, and, in the winter, ice fishing.

The other main industry and an alternative energy source are the wind turbines shown here. The foothills of southern Alberta are home to one of Canada's most productive wind energy regions.

My story

_____

_____

_____

_____

_____

_____

My photos / doodles / sketches

Cypress Hills Interprovincial Park

The park straddles the Saskatchewan / Alberta border in the southeast corner of Alberta.

The highest point in Cypress Hills is at Head of the Mountain in Alberta at 1466 meters (4810 feet).

Rising from the rolling prairie are steep hills, which create a plateau, lush valleys, and beautiful vistas.

The scenery is an outstanding testament to our reasons for travelling in Alberta.

Enjoy winter activities of cross-country skiing, ice fishing, skating, snowmobiling, snow shoeing. Summer recreation includes biking, hiking, boating, fishing, golfing, horseback riding, swimming, wind surfing, the list is endless.

Winter and summer camping is readily available.[5]

My story

_____

_____

_____

_____

_____

_____

My photos / doodles / sketches

More Sights Of Alberta

Here we have various buildings which emphasize the Calgary skyline, for example, the Calgary Tower, the Bow Building, Banker's Hall and the Saddle Dome, all nestled in front of our majestic Rockies.

My story

_____

_____

_____

_____

_____

_____

My photos / doodles / sketches

Canada Olympic Park

This is the main site of the 1988 Winter Olympics, which was hosted by Calgary, Alberta February 13 - 28, 1988. Venues located outside of the city are Nakiska Ski Area and the Canmore Nordic Centre. The Olympic Oval and the Olympic Saddle Dome are also offsite, but still within the city.

The Games are remembered for the "heroic failure" of British ski jumper Eddie "The Eagle" Edwards and the Winter Olympic debut of the Jamaican national bobsled team. Movies have been made about both "heroes."

The Calgary Games were, at the time, one of the most expensive winter Olympics ever held; however, the organizing committee turned record television and sponsorship revenue into a net surplus that was used to maintain the venues built for the Olympics and develop the Calgary region into the heart of Canada's elite winter sports program. The five purpose-built venues continue to be used in their original functions and helped Canada develop into one of the top nations in Winter Olympic competition; Canada more than quintupled the five medals it won in Calgary at the 2010 Games in Vancouver, the next Winter Olympics to be hosted on Canadian soil. Visit Canada Olympic Park to enjoy world-class sports facilities.

We have included the mascots, Howdy and Heidi, at the ski jump site at Canada Olympic Park.[6]

My story

_____

_____

_____

_____

_____

My photos / doodles / sketches

The Calgary Stampede, Bronco Busting

The Calgary Stampede attracts visitors from all corners of the world. There are 10 days to participate in rodeo, art exhibits, midway rides, stage presentations, and partake in the most interesting and bizarre combinations of food and drink.

Visitors and locals alike have enjoyed this annual fair/stampede since 1886 when the first roots of the official stampede were planted.

The most controversial and exciting events are the rodeo and chuckwagon races. The adrenaline is high and the crowd gets wild.

Wear your favorite cowboy boots, spurs, jeans, hat, and cowboy shirt and join the fun.

Yahoo, pardner!

My story

_____

_____

_____

_____

_____

_____

My photos / doodles / sketches

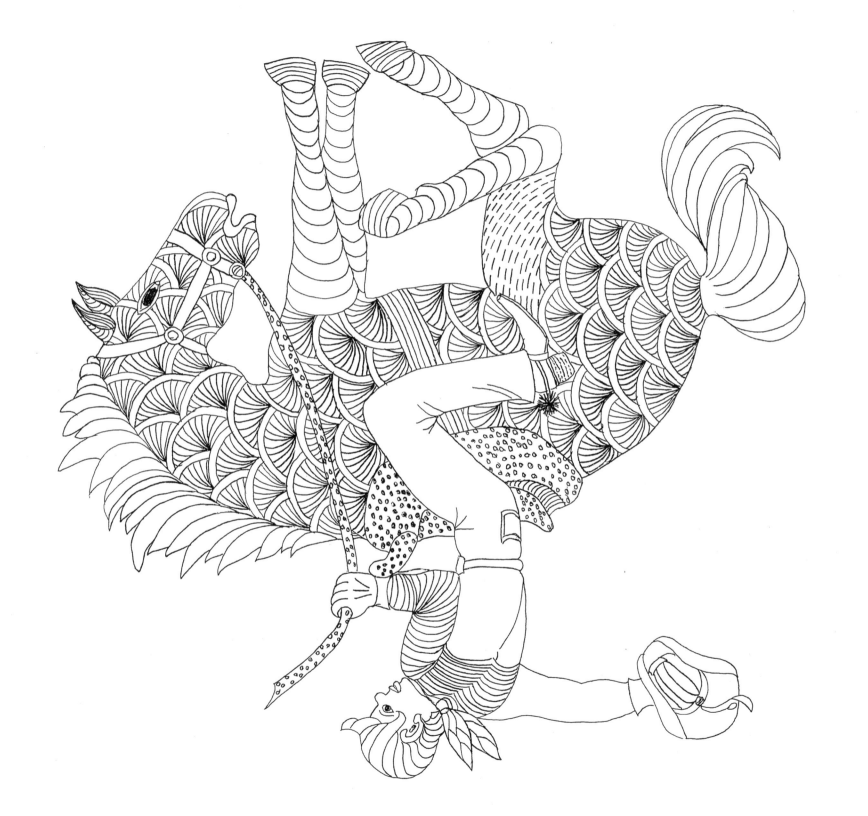

First Nations

Participation and representation of Alberta's First Nations people in all aspects of the Calgary Stampede remains one of its most unique components.

Enjoy touring Indian Village, learning of customs and historic culture, as well as catching up on current news issues. Spectacular displays of costumes, dancing and horsemanship are evident throughout the events.

My story

_____

_____

_____

_____

_____

_____

My photos / doodles / sketches

Horses, horses, horses, this is every little girl's dream come true. If you want to see horses of every description, the Calgary Stampede is the place for you. The Budweiser Clydesdales and their beautiful wagon have presented shows like no other for many years

My story

_____

_____

_____

_____

_____

_____

My photos / doodles / sketches

The pony on the next page is a pinto, or in, say our great grand-father's time, these ponies were known as "paints". This refers to their colouring versus their breed. The United States now has the greatest number of pinto horses in the world. Keep a sharp eye out and you will see a few pintos at the Stampede.

My story

_____

_____

_____

_____

_____

_____

My photos / doodles / sketches

The Chuckwagon Races. In some people's mind the Calgary Stampede would not be complete without the Chuckwagon Races. The wagons tear down the track with the Outriders in hot pursuit, adrenalin is high. The dust, sweat and mud filling the air. The outfits have four horses, unlike the next picture, where there are only two showing. Enjoy embellishing this picture to make it your own.

My story

_____

_____

_____

_____

_____

_____

My photos / doodles / sketches

Alberta Legislature Building

The Alberta Legislature Building is located in Edmonton, Alberta, and is the meeting place of the Legislative Assembly and the Executive Council. It is known to Edmontonians as "the Ledge."

The building is located on a promontory overlooking the North Saskatchewan River valley to the south, which was once the location of Fort Edmonton (1830-1915), a Hudson's Bay Company fur-trading post. It is just up the hill from the archaeological finds at Rossdale Flats to the east, which was a long-standing First Nations campsite. The Alberta Legislature Building location was selected by the first session of the Legislature shortly after Edmonton was confirmed as the provincial capital in 1906.

The use of Greek, Roman, and Egyptian architectural influences was considered appropriate for a public building, as they suggested power, permanence, and tradition. Beaux-Arts buildings are characterized by a large central dome above a spacious rotunda, a symmetrical T-shaped plan, doors and windows decorated with arches or lintels, and a portico supported by massive columns. The dome has terracotta made by Gibbs and Canning of Tamworth, Staffordshire, UK.

The building is supported on concrete piles and constructed around a steel skeleton. The first floor is faced with Vancouver Island granite; upper floors feature sandstone from the Glenbow Quarry in Calgary. The interior fittings include imported marble, mahogany, oak, and brass.

The building is about 57 metres (187 feet) in overall height and the project cost over $2 million at the time[7].

My story

_____

_____

_____

_____

_____

_____

My photos / doodles / sketches

Alberta's Oil Industry

Alberta's oil industry began in 1947 with the first major discovery near Leduc, just south of Edmonton.

Since that time the Alberta economy and many people have relied upon oil production for their livelihoods through boom and bust times.

This production has had a direct impact upon all Canadians with royalties and taxes contributing millions of dollars to the Canadian Treasury. With the current affairs of world oil production and market availability, the oil industry and all those associated with this industry are suffering significant economic loss. However, as in the past, times will get better.

My story

_____

_____

_____

_____

_____

_____

My photos / doodles / sketches

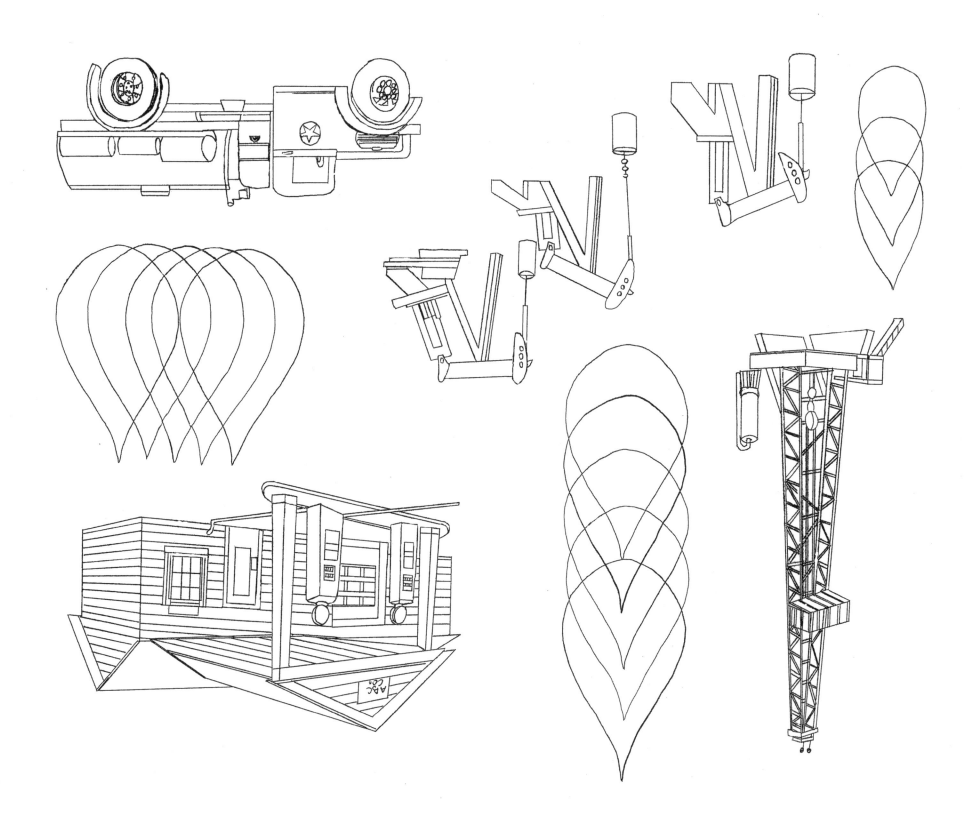

The Great Horned Owl

My husband worked in renovation construction on a project in Northwest Calgary. Everyday at dawn and dusk we would hear the hooting of an owl, but he/she was elusive, we couldn't see the beast!

A neighbour, Mr. Abe, pointed out the beautiful pair of great horned owls who have lived in the area for more than 20 years and they have nested in the same large poplar tree every year.

Here are a few silly lines to tell you about this bird:

Known as Alberta's official provincial bird, the long tufted "ears" can look quite absurd.

Ho-hum colours of gray, white, beige, and brown, the wise old Owl, frowns sternly down.

This Great Horned Owl didn't eat honey and he didn't use a pea green boat to go to sea. He lives in the top of a 50-foot tree.

A foot and a half wide and 2 feet long, haunting hoot, hoots are definitely his song.

His eyes are keen, he can see for miles. Dinner is served by his wits, not smiles.

I've had the pleasure to see a life long pair, living in the city without a care.

My story

_____

_____

_____

_____

_____

_____

My photos / doodles / sketches

Bobcat

You may think you have seen movement just off the trail you are hiking. All that remains is a shadow in the forest's under-growth. The hair on the back of your neck is standing up and you feel a watchful eye looking in your direction. You may have encountered Alberta's rare bobcat.

My grandfather's career had him walking miles of pipeline along the right-of-way in the 1930s and 1940s checking for gas leaks. One of his stories was how a bobcat tracked and hunted him for over a week. Gramps only saw him once or twice, but he knew that the cat was hot on his trail all day long, just waiting for an opportunity to strike. Nothing disastrous ever happened to Grandpa, the Bobcat found smaller and easier prey, perhaps a rabbit or squirrel. When Grandpa told his bobcat story he always made the experience exciting and scary for us, and always just before bedtime.

My story

_____

_____

_____

_____

_____

_____

My photos / doodles / sketches

Moose

Moose are the largest of all the deer species, standing 1.5 to 2 meters (5 - 6.5 feet) high. They are amazingly huge. Resembling a horse, their gait is long and they cover miles of countryside in a single day. We have two female moose with calves who regularly amble through our yard, pulling at all the tasty willow bushes, flowering crabapple, and dogwood shrubs. The moose family of mothers and calves stay together for two summers when the calves are old enough to fend for themselves.

One of our neighbours has a deep pond on their property, which the moose love. They feed on the aquatic plants at the bottom, staying in the pond all day and taking possession of the property. The neighbour has difficulty enjoying their yard, however, they do get to witness moose behaviour up close and personal.

My story

_____
_____
_____
_____
_____
_____

My photos / doodles / sketches

Bears

There are two species of bear in Alberta, the grizzly bear and the black bear.

Some years when the snow melts early, the warm weather interrupts hibernation. The hungry, grumpy bears are soon up looking for grass, flowers, insects, and carrion left by winter's harshness.

Looks like this bear has found some honey

Grizzly bears:

- have a pronounced hump on their shoulders
- may have silver or light-tipped guard hairs on their head, shoulder hump, and back
- can range in colour from blonde to black
- have rounded, smallish ears
- have pig-like noses
- have long claws (7.5-10 cm), which may have a light-coloured strip

Black bears:

- appear more uniform in colour
- can range in colour from blonde to black
- have pointed, prominent ears
- have dog-like noses
- have short claws[8] (2.5 cm), which are usually black

My story

_____

_____

_____

_____

_____

_____

_____

My photos / doodles / sketches

Bunny Rabbits

Once again, here are some silly lines to tell you about the rabbits and bunnies in Alberta.

Cottontail, Cottontail where have you been? I've been to Canmore to visit my feral friends.

Jack Rabbit, Jack Rabbit, what did you there? I went to compete in the Highland Games fair.

Bunny Rabbit, Bunny Rabbit what did you eat? I dined on grass, buds, twigs, and bark off the trees. My tummy is full, thank-you, please.

Snowshoe Hare, Snowshoe Hare, who did you meet? I met cross-country skiers at the Nordic Centre - they're fast on their feet. I didn't meet the Queen, but now you know where I've been.

My story

_____

_____

_____

_____

_____

_____

My photos / doodles / sketches

Bighorn Sheep

Bighorn sheep are majestic Rocky Mountain dwellers and are part of the amazing ambiance of the mountain life.

Hopefully, you have or will have the opportunity to see these beauties in person - but not too close!

My story

_____

_____

_____

_____

_____

_____

My photos / doodles / sketches

Fish of Alberta

There are 63 species of fish in Alberta; however, only 17 are preferred by anglers and considered "game fish."

Here are eight of those preferred fish:

Arctic char
Walleye
Lake sturgeon
Rainbow trout
Brook trout
Yellow perch
Golden trout
Cutthroat trout

My story

_____

_____

_____

_____

_____

_____

My photos / doodles / sketches

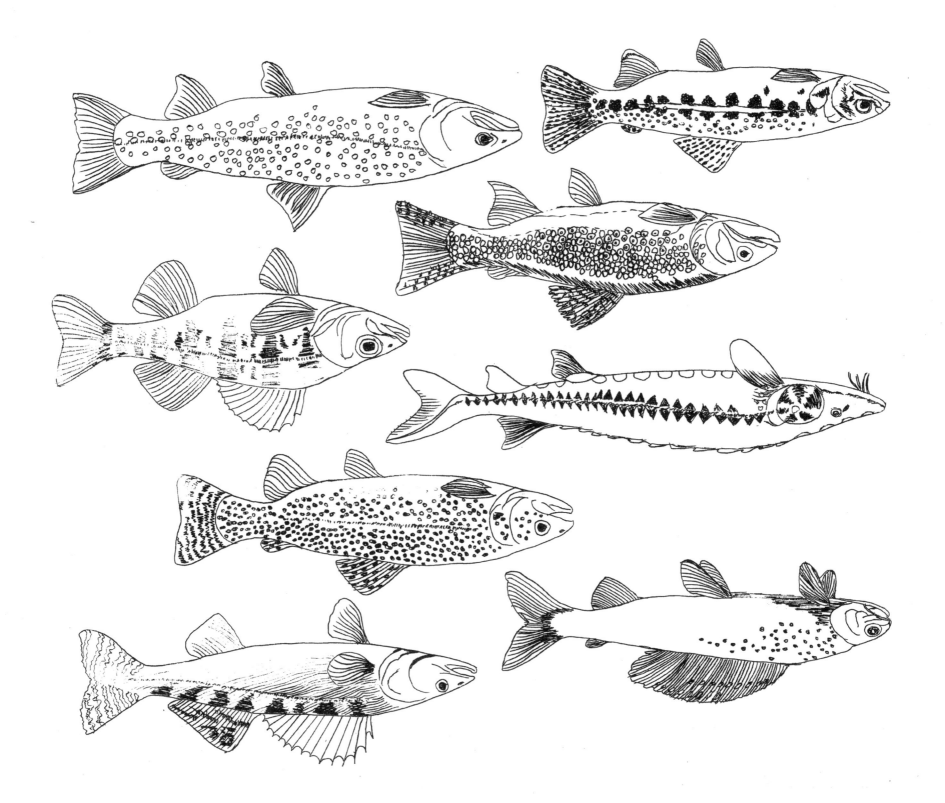

Butterflies and Ants

On the next two pages we have shown butterflies, ants, dragon-flies, ladybugs, and bumble bees.

Some of the butterflies are:

Canadian Tiger Swallowtail
White Admiral
Northern Crescent,
Silvery-blue,
Meadow Fritillary

And a Monarch on the following page.

The other insects are generally found everywhere in Canada and are mostly beneficial in nature.

My story

_____

_____

_____

_____

_____

_____

_____

My photos / doodles / sketches

My story

_____

_____

_____

_____

_____

_____

_____

_____

_____

_____

_____

_____

_____

_____

_____

My photos / doodles / sketches

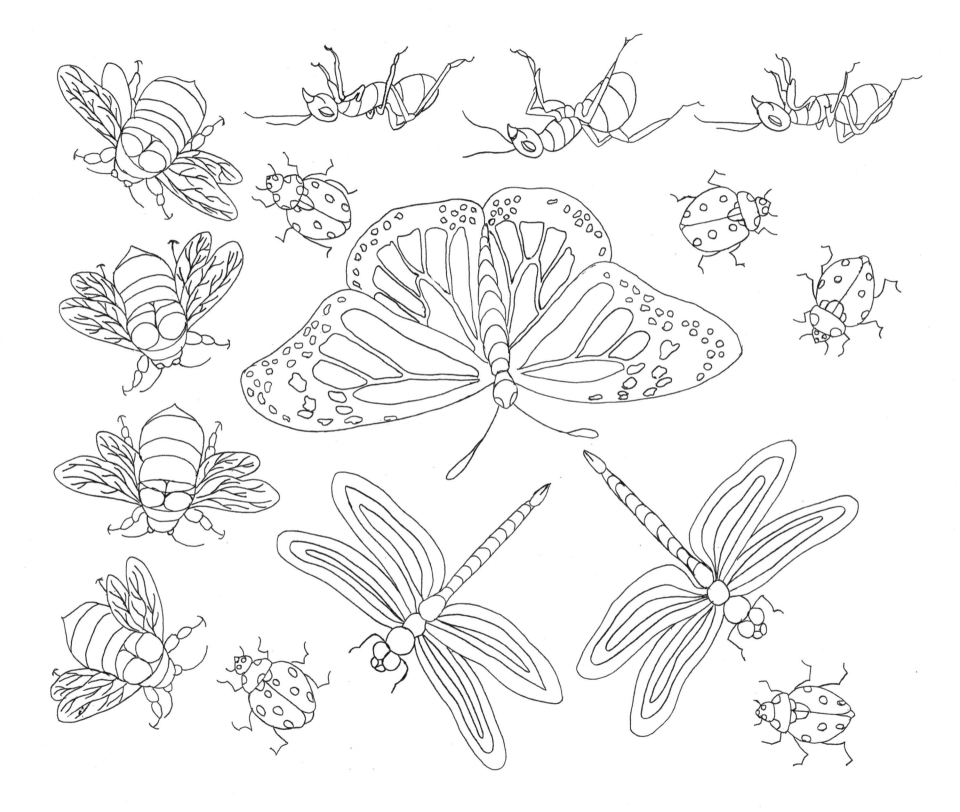

Loon

Adults can range from 61-100 cm (24-40 in) in length with a 122-152 cm (4-5-ft) wingspan. The weight can vary from 1.6 to 8 kg (3.6 to 17.6 lbs).

As an International competing woodcarver, a Loon is positively the largest most beautiful realistic bird I have had the pleasure to create.

With an average length of 75 cm. (30 inches) and a 140 cm (4½ foot) wingspan they are truly majestic.

We can all relate to the lonely, haunting call of a loon at dusk, echoing across the lake, it's almost heart breaking. I saw my first real live Loon on the reservoir in Canmore, a lovely female, with a single chick nestled into the feathers on her back, staying high and dry. We checked on her a few times throughout the summer, watched her fish and feed her baby, then one day they were gone, the cycle continues.[9]

My story

_____
_____
_____
_____
_____
_____

My photos / doodles / sketches

Wolf

Alberta can boast some of the largest and most handsome of all wolves, which belong to the *Canis lupus occidentalis* group. They are mostly confined to the Rocky Mountains, foothills, and boreal forest regions. Present-day wolves are estimated to number around 4,000 in Alberta.

The grey wolf is the largest member of the wild dog family. An adult may weigh up to 60 kilograms (130 pounds). Fur is commonly grey with dark shading, but may vary in colour from near black to almost white. Coats are long and dense. The face is broad with a muzzle that is less pointed than a coyote's. The ears are thickly furred. Large feet aid in travelling over snow.

Wolves are social animals found in packs numbering from 2 to over 20. Pack size tends to be largest in winter.

Grey wolf territories can range from 250 - 750 square kilometres (97 - 282 square miles). The wolf's howl helps wolves communicate across long distances and also helps to establish pack territories.[10]

My story

_____

_____

_____

_____

_____

_____

My photos / doodles / sketches

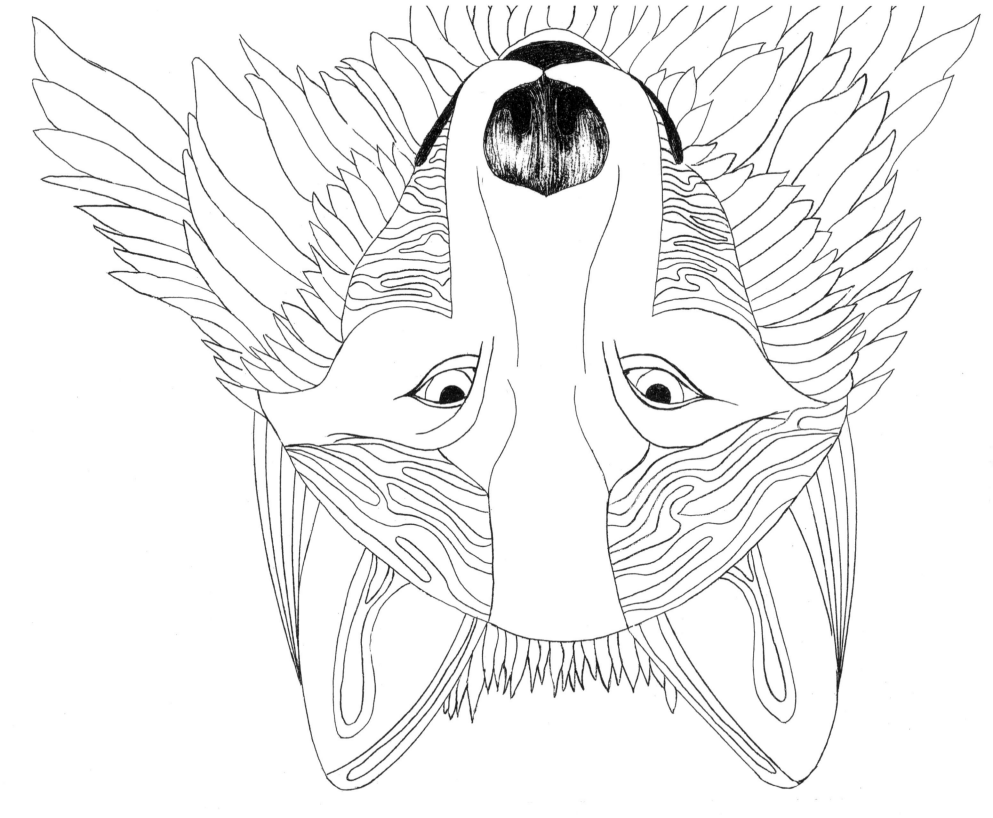

Modes of transporation to take you on your travelling experiences:

This is not the end, but the beginning of your next travel experience.

We hope you have enjoyed our presentation of Alberta, Canada.

Thank you for giving us this pleasure.

My story

_____

_____

_____

_____

_____

_____

_____

My photos / doodles / sketches

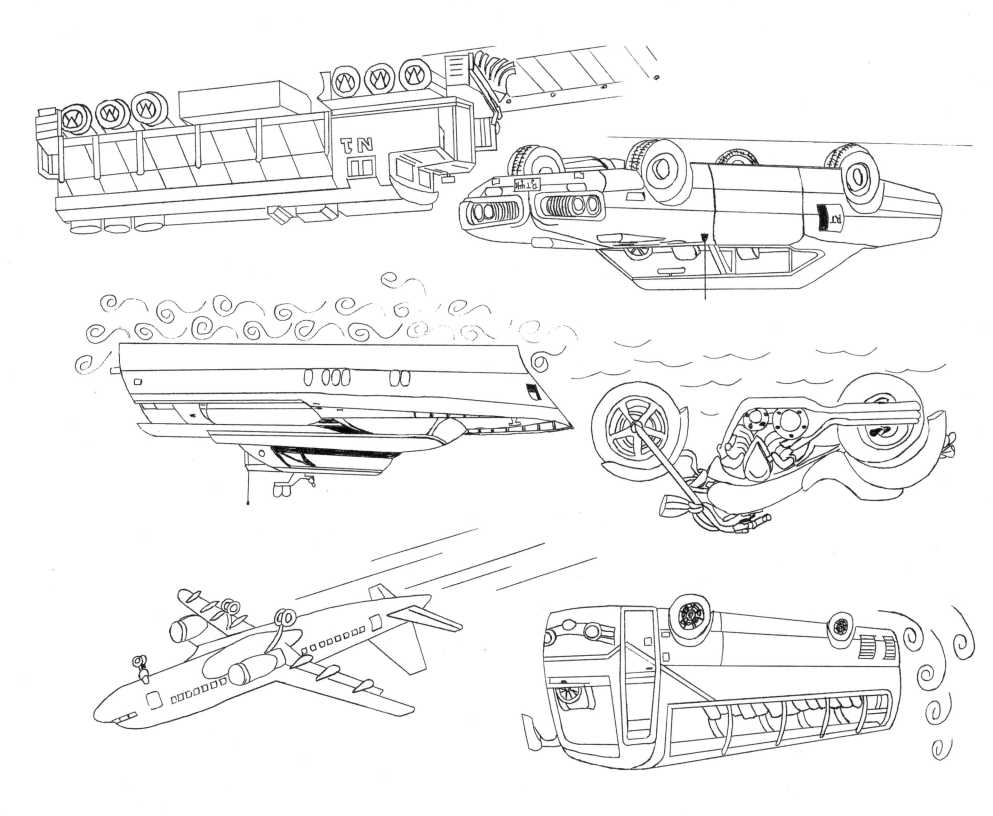

Endnotes

1   https://en.wikipedia.org/wiki/Alberta; accessed March 1, 2016.

2   https://en.m.wikipedia.org/wiki/Three_Sisters_(Alberta); accessed March 1, 2016.

3   https://en.m.wikipedia.org/wiki/Three_Sisters_(Alberta); accessed March 1, 2016

4   https://en.wikipedia.org/wiki/Southern_Alberta; accessed March 1, 2016

5   https://en.wikipedia.org/wiki/Cypress_Hills_Interprovincial_Park; accessed March 1, 2016

6   https://en.wikipedia.org/wiki/1988_Winter_Olympics; accessed March 1, 2016

7   https://en.wikipedia.org/wiki/Alberta_Legislature_Building; accessed March 1, 2016

8   https://en.m.wikipedia.org/wiki Bears in Alberta; accessed March 1, 2016

9   https://en.m.wikipedia.org/wiki Loons in Alberta; accessed March 1, 2016

10   https://albertawilderness.ca/issues/wildlife/wolves/ accessed; March 1, 2016